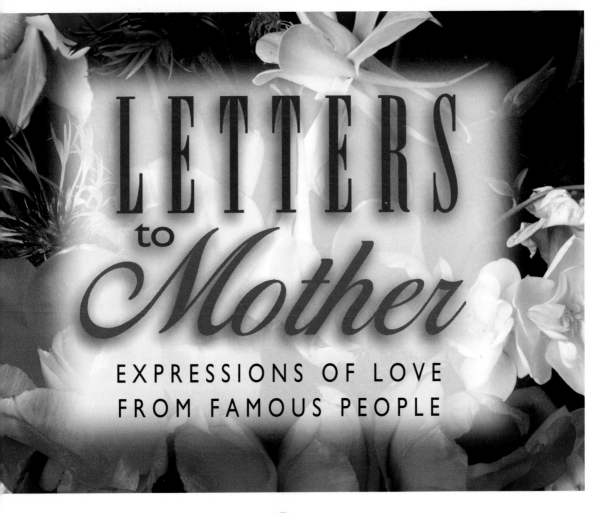

LETTERS
to
Mother

EXPRESSIONS OF LOVE
FROM FAMOUS PEOPLE

PENBROOKE
PUBLISHING

Tulsa, Oklahoma

ISBN 1-889116-00-9

Printed in the United States of America

First U.S. Edition

Design by Paragon Communications Group, Inc., Tulsa, Oklahoma

Published by

PENBROOKE PUBLISHING

Tulsa, Oklahoma

ACKNOWLEDGMENTS

Alcott, Louisa May: *Life, Letters and Journals,* compiled and edited by Ednah D. Cheney, Random House Publishers. **Branch, Anna Hempstead:** *The Shoes That Danced and Other Poems* by Anna Hempstead Branch, Houghton Mifflin Company, 1905. **Brandeis, Louis:** *Brandeis: A Free Man's Life* by Alpheus Thomas Mason. Reprinted by permission of George Allen & Unwin, an imprint of HarperCollins Publishers Limited. **Dinesen, Isak:** *Letters From Africa,* published by The University of Chicago Press, 1981; originally published in two volumes. Copyright © 1978 The Rungstedlund Foundation. Reprinted by permission of The University of Chicago Press. **Flaubert, Gustave:** *Gustave Flaubert Letters,* selected by Richard Rumbold and translated by J. M. Cohen. George Weidenfeld and Nicolson Limited. Reprinted by permission of the Orion Publishing Group Limited. **Johnson, Samuel:** *The Letters of Samuel Johnson,* vol. 1, edited by Bruce Redford. Copyright © 1991 by Princeton University Press. Reprinted by permission of Princeton University Press. **Mansfield, Katherine:** © The Estate of Katherine Mansfield 1984. Reprinted from *The Collected Letters of Katherine Mansfield, vol. 1 1903-1917* (1984) by permission of Oxford University Press. **Millay, Edna St. Vincent:** Excerpt from letter of Edna St. Vincent Millay to Mrs. Cora B. Millay, 1921. Letter #28, *Letters of Edna St. Vincent Millay,* Harper & Row. © 1952, 1980 by Norma Millay Ellis. Reprinted by permission of Elizabeth Barnett, literary executor. **Plath, Sylvia:** *Letters Home by Sylvia Plath: Correspondence 1950-1963* by Aurelia Schober Plath. Copyright © 1975 by Aurelia Schober Plath. Reprinted by permission of HarperCollins Publishers, Inc. **Proust, Marcel:** *Marcel Proust: Selected Letters 1880-1903,* edited by Philip Kolb, translated by Ralph Mannheim. Translation copyright © 1983 by William Collins Sons and Co. and Doubleday, a division of Bantam Doubleday Dell Publishing Group, Inc. Used by permission of Doubleday, a division of Bantam Doubleday Dell Publishing Group, Inc. **Royal Air Force Pilot:** *The Englishman's Religion* by Ashley Sampton. Reprinted by permission of George Allen & Unwin, an imprint of HarperCollins Publishers Limited. **Sand, George:** *Letters of George Sand,* edited by Veronica Lucas, Houghton Mifflin Publishers. Reprinted by permission of Routledge and Kegan, London. **Wagner, Richard:** *Family Letters of Richard Wagner,* translated by William Ashton Ellis, Macmillan and Company Limited.

Presented to:

_____

From:

_____

Date:

_____

My Mother's Clothes

When I was small, my mother's clothes
All seemed so kind to me!
I hid my face amid the folds
As safe as safe could be.

The gown that she had on
To me seemed shining bright,
For woven in that simple stuff
Were comfort and delight.

Yes, everything she wore
Received my hopes and fears,
And even the garments of her soul
Contained my smiles and tears.

Then softly I will touch
This dress she used to wear.
The old-time comfort lingers yet,
My smiles and tears are there.

A tenderness abides
Though laid so long away,
And I must kiss their empty folds,
So comfortable are they.

—Anna Hempstead Branch

LOUISA MAY ALCOTT

Louisa May Alcott

Louisa May Alcott, best known for the
largely autobiographical, Little Women, was the
second of four daughters born to Bronson and
Abigail Alcott. The family's close ties of friendship to
leading Transcendentalists such as Henry David Thoreau
immersed young Louisa in a highly developed intellectual
world. While she enjoyed things of this nature, her real passion
grew from writing the beloved story of the March sisters, as well
as many other popular novels. Louisa's writing career brought
her wide recognition and financially stabilized her struggling
family. The following letter to her mother is in regard to her
book of short stories entitled Flower Fables. It became
Louisa's first published work in 1860.

We are together, my child and I.
Mother and child, yes, but sisters really, against
whatever denies us all that we are.
—Alice Walker

20 Pinckney Street, Boston, Dec. 25, 1854
[With Flower Fables]

Dear Mother, — Into your Christmas stocking I have put my "first-born," knowing that you will accept it with all its faults (for grandmothers are always kind), and look upon it merely as an earnest of what I may yet do; for, with so much to cheer me on, I hope to pass in time from fairies and fables to men and realities.

Whatever beauty of poetry is to be found in my little book is owing to your interest in and encouragement of all my efforts from the first to the last; and if ever I do anything to be proud of, my greatest happiness will be that I can thank you for that, as I may do for all the good there is in me; and I shall be content to write if it gives you pleasure.

Jo is fussing about;
My lamp is going out.

To dear mother, with many kind wishes
for a happy New Year and merry
Christmas.

I am ever your loving daughter,
Louy

Mother's Knee

What is so wondrous as mother's knee?
Where so delightful a spot can be?
Beautiful garden, where children play,
Romping and laughing the livelong day;
There are sung all of our nursery rhymes,
And little ones have all the best of times.
A wonderful playground is mother's knee,
The best place on earth for a child to be.
What is so wondrous as mother's knee?
When night comes, it's the place to be;
No longer a playground it is at night,
But a drowsy cradle, soft and white,
That gently swings, until it seems
Like a fairy ship on the sea of dreams;
Oh, a mother's knee is the place that's best
When a weary baby wants a rest.
But age creeps on and we grown-ups see
No longer the haven of mother's knee;
When weary and faint with our weight of woe,
We've no such comforting place to go.
When night time comes we must sink to rest,
With our troubled brows still uncaressed;
And we'd give our all once again to be
A child once more at our mother's knee.

–Edgar A. Guest

There is only one pretty child in the world, & every mother has it.
—English Proverb

———

Some are kissing mothers and some are scolding mothers, but it is love just the same, and most mothers kiss and scold together.
—Pearl S. Buck

———

A mother is she who can take the place of all others, but whose place no one else can take.
—Cardinal Mermillod

Richard Wagner

Richard Wagner

Richard Wagner, one of the greatest composers of
German opera had relatively little training in
comparison with the volume of work he introduced and
the fullness of its appreciation. His works include the
early Shakespearean influenced, The Fairies, and the
somewhat popular Forbidden Love. His most well-
known work is the Flying Dutchman, which received
much recognition. Wagner died in 1883 leaving behind
a vast collection of musical achievements.

Romance fails us — and so do friendships — but the
relationship of Mother and Child remains indelible and
indestructible — the strongest bond upon this earth.
—Theodor Reik

Carlsbad, the 25th July: 35.

Only of yourself, dearest Mother, can I think with the sincerest love and profoundest emotion. Brothers and sisters, I know it, must go their own way, —each has an eye to himself, to his future, and the surroundings connected to both. So it is, and I feel it myself: there comes a time when roads part of themselves, —when our mutual relations are governed solely from the standpoint of external life; we become more nodding diplomats to one another, keeping silence where silence seems politic, and speaking where our view of an affair demands; and when we're at a distance from each other, we speak the most. But ah, how high a mother's love is poised above all that!

Mother—now I have left you, the feeling of thanks for that grand love of yours towards your child, which you displayed to him so warmly and so tenderly again the other day, so overpowers me that I fain would write, nay, tell you of it in accents soft as of a lover to his sweetheart. Yes, and still softer, —for is not a mother's love far more —far more untainted than all other?

Nay, here I won't philosophize, —I simply want to thank you, and again, to thank you. . . .

To My Mother

Because I feel that, in the Heavens above,
The angels, whispering to one another,
Can find, among their burning terms of love,
None so devotional as that of "Mother,"
Therefore by that dear name I long to have called you—
You who are more than mother unto me,
And fill my heart of hearts, where Death installed you,
In setting my Virginia's spirit free.
My mother—my own mother, who died early,
Was but the mother of myself; but you
Are mother to the one I loved so dearly,
And thus are dearer than the mother I knew
By that infinity with which my wife
Was dearer to my soul than its soul-life.
—Edgar Allan Poe

Mother means selfless devotion,
& limitless sacrifice,
love that passes understanding.

—Anonymous

With what a price we pay
for the
glory of motherhood.

—Isadora Duncan

If you bungle raising your children,
I don't think whatever else
you do well matters very much.

— Jacqueline Kennedy Onassis

One *good mother* is
worth a hundred school masters.

—George Herbert

Edna St. Vincent Millay

Edna St. Vincent Millay

Edna St. Vincent Millay was a Pulitzer Prize winning American poet and widely recognized sonneteer. She was first published in 1917 and continued writing until her death in 1950. Among her collection of writings exists a wealth of letters to her mother, Cora Millay, for whom Edna had a tender affection. The following letter is one example of the devotion Edna shared with her mother.

My mother wanted me to be her wings,
to fly as she never quite had the courage to do.
I love her for that. I love that she
wanted to give birth to her own wings.
–Erica Jong

Hôtel de l'Intendance
[June 15, 1921]
50, rue de l'Université, Paris.

Dearly Beloved:

. . .It is nearly six months now since I saw you. A long time. Mother, do you know, almost all people love their mothers, but I have never met anybody in my life, I think, who loved his mother as much as I love you. I don't believe there ever was anybody who did, quite so much, and quite in so many wonderful ways. I was telling somebody yesterday that the reason I am a poet is entirely because you wanted me to be and intended I should be, even from the very first. You brought me up in the tradition of poetry, and everything I did you encouraged. I can not remember once in my life when you were not interested in what I was working on, or even suggested that I should put it aside for something else. Some parents of children that are "different" have so much to reproach themselves with. But not you great spirit.

I hope you will write me as soon as you get this. If you only knew what it means to me to get letters from any of you. . .over there. Because no matter how interesting it all is, and how beautiful, and how happy I am, and how much work I get done, I am nevertheless away from home, —home being somewhere near where you are, mother dear.

If I didn't keep calling you mother, anybody reading this would think I was writing to my sweetheart. And he would be quite right.

. . .Well, dear, this is enough for now. I will write again soon. And you write me. And believe me to be as ever, honored parent, your most obedient humble servant and devoted daughter,

Vincent.

A Valentine to My Mother

My blessed Mother dozing in her chair
On Christmas Day seemed an embodied Love,
A comfortable Love with soft brown hair
Softened and silvered to a tint of dove;
A better sort of Venus with an air
Angelical from thoughts that dwell above;
A wiser Pallas in whose body fair
Enshrined a blessed soul looks out thereof.
Winter brought holly then; now Spring has brought
Paler and frailer snowdrops shivering;
And I have brought a simple humble thought—
I her duteous Valentine—
A lifelong thought which drills this song I sing,
A lifelong love to this dear saint of mine.

—Christina Rossetti

A mother has, *perhaps, the hardest earthly lot; and yet no mother* **worthy of the name** *ever* **gave herself thoroughly** *for her child who did not feel that, after all, she reaped what she had sown.*

— Henry Ward Beecher

There is no influence so powerful as that of the **mother.**

—Sarah Hale

Mothers are made of tenderness, & sweet sleep blesses the child who lies therein.

—Victor Hugo

SAMUEL JOHNSON

Samuel Johnson

Samuel Johnson, often thought of as one of the greatest men of letters in English literature, left behind a rich legacy. He displayed remarkable diversity in the offices of essayist, lexicographer (dictionary writer), poet and critic, garnering much admiration during the second half of the eighteenth century. Johnson has been esteemed as a moralist and is particularly noted for his criticism of the works of William Shakespeare. Throughout his life, Johnson maintained a close relationship with his mother. This letter was written as she lay on her deathbed in 1759.
He died in London in 1784.

The woman who creates and sustains a home, and under whose hands children grow up to be strong and pure men and women is a creator second only to God.
— Helen Hunt Jackson

26

Jan. 20, 1759

Dear honored Mother,

. . .You have been the best mother, and I believe the best woman in the world. I thank you for your indulgence to me, and beg forgiveness of all that I have done ill, and all that I have omitted to do well. God grant you his Holy Spirit, and receive you to everlasting happiness, for Jesus Christ's sake. Amen. Lord Jesus receive your spirit. Amen. I am, dear, dear, Mother, your dutiful son.

Sam Johnson

❧ *A Virtuous Woman* ❧

Who can find a virtuous woman? For her price is far above rubies.

The heart of her husband doth safely trust in her, so that he shall not need of spoil.

She will do him good and not evil all the days of her life.

She stretcheth out her hand to the poor; yea she reacheth forth her hands to the needy.

Strength and honor are her clothing; and she shall rejoice in time to come.

She openeth her mouth with wisdom; and in her tongue is the law of kindness.

She looketh well to the ways of her household, and eateth not the bread of idleness.

Her children arise up, and call her blessed; her husband also, and he praiseth her.

—Proverbs 31:10-12, 19, 25-28

A mother understands what
a child **does not say.**

– Jewish Proverb

A suburban mother's role
is to deliver **children** *obstetrically* once,
and by car *forever* after.

– Peter De Vries

Mothers are like *fine*
collectibles – they **increase** in
value as the years go by.

– Anonymous

ISAK DINESEN

Isak Dinesen

The Baroness Karen Blixen-Finecke, otherwise known as Danish short story writer Isak Dinesen (1885-1962), is most famous for her detailed accounts of life in Africa. She may be best known for her semi-autobiographical work, *Out of Africa*, which was made into a critically acclaimed film. Dinesen lived on and managed a coffee plantation in East Africa for many years, throughout which she maintained a close relationship with her mother. The following letter was written shortly after one of her mother's visits.

When God thought of Mother, he must have laughed with satisfaction, and framed it quickly —so rich, so deep, so divine, so full of soul, power, and beauty, was the conception.

—Henry Ward Beecher

My beloved blessed Mother,

From the moment when I saw your beloved face disappear in the train I have been looking forward every single day to seeing it again on the veranda at Rungsted, and after all that is not so far off. . .When I got back here to the farm I felt that the sense of loss was almost too hard to bear; but as I turned the corner and the house came in sight a strange thing happened: I felt as if I were coming home to you, and that is how it has been ever since, and still is. Now I can really understand what it means to say that the house where my mother has been is "forever blessed," and how true that is. You are on the veranda and on the stone bench. You are sitting in the drawing room sewing and coming out of your room to meet me. Everything that I have been attached to has taken on a wonderful new value because your eyes have rested on it and because you care for it. I can never be alone in this house again. . . .

I have nothing else to write about today. I want to thank you once more, thousands and thousands of times, for coming out here; I will never, never forget that you did that. From the very first moment when I unexpectedly saw your face in the car to the final minute, the hours and days seem like a huge rich treasure that I have gathered together and can never, never lose. . .Dearest, dearest Mother, now as I am writing and as I look up I seem to see you standing there, and hear your steps and your voice and feel that you must be in the house and so you are; "The power of the spirit is great" one knows that and yet one goes on thinking in doctrinal terms of physical conditions and suffers for it. . .Thanks and thanks and thanks again, as long as I live, for coming.

Your Tanne.

To My Mother

They tell us of an Indian tree
    Which howso'er the sun and sky
    May tempt its boughs to wander free,
    And shoot and blossom, wide and high,
    Far better love to bend its arms
    Downward again to that dear earth
    From which the life, that fills and warms
    Its grateful being, first had birth.
    'Tis thus, though wooed by flattering friends,
    And fed with fame (if fame may be),
    This heart, my own dear mother, bends,
    With love's true instinct, back to thee!

    – Thomas Moore

What the mother sings to the cradle goes all the way down to the coffin.

—Henry Ward Beecher

A mother is a person who sees that there are only four pieces of pie for five persons and promptly remarks that she's never cared for pie.

—Anonymous

All that I am, or hope to be, I owe to my angel mother.

—Abraham Lincoln

35

GEORGE SAND

George Sand

Aurore Dudevant, under the pseudonym George Sand, became the most famous female writer in nineteenth century France. Unhappily married to a Baron, Sand left her husband and took up writing in order to support herself and her two children. Her early novels such as *Valentine* and *Lelia* are somewhat autobiographical as they express the hardships of escaping a difficult marriage. Later works divulge her passion for politics and a heartfelt interest in the events of the French Revolution. George Sand eventually retired to her estate at Nohant where she died in 1876.

I remember my mother's prayers and they
have always followed me.
They have clung to me all of my life.
—Abraham Lincoln

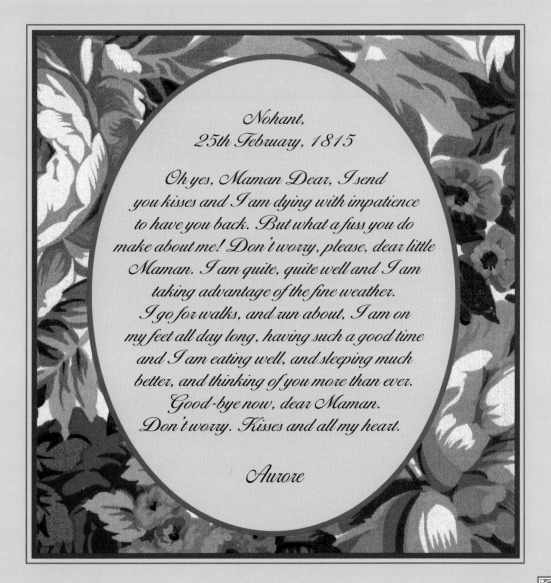

Nohant,
25th February, 1815

Oh yes, Maman Dear, I send
you kisses and I am dying with impatience
to have you back. But what a fuss you do
make about me! Don't worry, please, dear little
Maman. I am quite, quite well and I am
taking advantage of the fine weather.
I go for walks, and run about, I am on
my feet all day long, having such a good time
and I am eating well, and sleeping much
better, and thinking of you more than ever.
Good-bye now, dear Maman.
Don't worry. Kisses and all my heart.

Aurore

Mother

As long ago we carried to your knees

The tales and treasures of eventful days,

Knowing no deed too humble for your praise,

Nor any gift too trivial to please,

So still we bring with older smiles and tears,

What gifts we may to claim the old, dear right;

Your faith beyond the silence and the night;

Your love still close and watching

through the years.

—Anonymous

A Mother is the thread that mends a broken heart.

—Anonymous

Youth fades;
love droops,
the leaves of friendship fall:
A mother's secret hope
outlives them all.

—Oliver Wendell Holmes

A hundred men may
make an encampment,
but it takes a woman
to make a home.

—Chinese Proverb

Dear Mother—You know
that nothing can ever change
what we have always been and
always will be to each other.

—Franklin Roosevelt, 1911

HENRI DE TOULOUSE-LAUTREC

Henri de Toulouse-Lautrec

Henri de Toulouse-Lautrec was a leading Post-Impressionist artist who contributed much to the development of Art Nouveau in late nineteenth century France. His paintings, lithography and posters evoked contemporary Parisian nightlife through the exaggeration of shape, light and color. As a young boy, Toulouse-Lautrec suffered from the effects of bone disease which left him with crippling injuries to his legs. His tight-knit aristrocratic family was extremely supportive of him. The following letter to his mother was written at the age of 11, while he was away at school.

A mother is not a person to lean on,
but a person to make leaning unnecessary.
— Dorothey Canfield Fisher

Neuilly 22 September 75

My dear Mamma,

I was very glad of receiving such a pretty letter and I will tell you very good news. My Greek master was very satisfied with me and he put on a piece of paper "I am very satisfied of the lessons as well of the tasks." He gave me a Latin version to do. I have read my Latin Grammar this morning and I am going to do Miss' tasks. Yesterday I went to the bath and I have looked for the plate. M. Verrier was very satisfied with my legs. When you return I hope you will find me well. Give my love to every one and return soon. I finish my letter by telling you that everybody sends you his compliments and particularly your boy who kisses you 1000000000000000 million times.

Your affectionate boy,

Coco de Lautrec

My kiss

Child and Mother

O Mother-My Love, if you'll give me your hand
And go where I ask you to wander,
I will lead you away to a beautiful land—
The dreamland that's waiting out yonder.
We'll walk in the sweet posie gardens out there,
Where moonlight and starlight are streaming,
And the flowers and the birds are filling the air
With the fragrance and music of dreaming.

There'll be no little, tired-out boy to undress,
No questions or cares to perplex you;
There'll be no little bruises or bumps to caress,
Nor patchings of stockings to vex you.
For I'll rock you away on the silver-dew stream
And sing you asleep when you're weary,
And no one shall know of our beautiful dream,
But you and your own little dearie.

So, Mother-my-Love, let me take your dear hand
And away through the starlight we'll wander—
Away through the mist to that beautiful land—
The dreamland that's waiting out yonder.

—Eugene Field

There is no slave out of heaven
like a loving woman; and of all
loving women, there is no
such slave as a mother.
—Henry Ward Beecher

The common fallacy among women is
that simply having children
makes one a mother—
which is as absurd as believing that having a
piano makes one a musician.
—Sydney J. Harris

MARGARET FLEMING

Margaret Fleming

Margaret Fleming was a precocious eight-year-old poet who completely enamored Sir Walter Scott and other literary notables of her time. She wrote many letters and poems in her short life and managed to have a remarkable effect on everyone she came in contact with. This charming letter to her beloved mother, written while she was away at school, is characteristic of her warmth and personality.

❀   ❀   ❀

A mother's love is patient and forgiving
when all others are forsaking, and it never fails or falters,
even though the heart is breaking.
— Helen Steiner Rice

September 1811

My dear little Mama,

I was truly happy to hear that you were all well, we are surrounded by measles at present on every side. . . . I have begun dancing but am not very fond of it, for the boys strike and mock me — I have been another night at the dancing; I like it better. I will write to you as often as I can; but I am afraid not every week. I long for you with the longings of a child to embrace you — to hold you in my arms. I respect you with all the respect due to a mother. You don't know how I love you. So I shall remain, your loving child,

M. Fleming

Sonnets Are Full of Love, And This My Tome

Sonnets are full of love, and this my tome
Has many sonnets: so here now shall be
One sonnet more, a love sonnet, from me
To her whose heart is my heart's quiet home,
To my first Love, my Mother, on whose knee
I learnt love-lore that is not troublesome;
Whose service is my special dignity,
And she my loadstar while I go and come.
And so because you love me, and because
I love you, Mother, I have woven a wreath
Of rhymes wherewith to crown your honored name:
In you not fourscore years can dim the flame
Of love, whose blessed glow transcends the laws
Of time and change and mortal life and death.

—Christina Rossetti

Every mother is like Moses.
She does not enter the promised land.
She prepares a world she will not see.

—Pope Paul

Many make the household
but only one the home.

—James Russell Lowell

The mother's heart
is the child's
schoolroom.

—Henry Ward Beecher

ℛOYAL
AIR FORCE PILOT

R.A.F. Pilot

British Royal Air Force officers during
World War II very often sent letters home while in
the midst of serving their country. They are some of the
most intimate and loving writings that exist today. This
letter, found among the personal belongings of a bomber
pilot, reported missing and presumed dead, is one example of
such a letter. It is a testimony to the bond between mother and
child, a bond which cannot be broken even in the midst of war.

Beautiful as seemed mama's face,
it became incomparably more lovely
when she smiled, and seemed to
enliven everything about her.
– Leo Tolstoy

Dearest Mother,

Though I feel no premonition at all, events are moving rapidly, and I have instructed that this letter be forwarded to you should I fail to return from one of the raids which we shall shortly be called upon to undertake. You must hope on for a month, but at the end of that time you must accept the fact that I have handed my task over to the extremely capable hands of the Royal Air Force, as so many splendid fellows have already done.

First it will comfort you to know that my role in this war has been of the greatest importance. . . Though it will be difficult for you, you will disappoint me if you do not at least try to accept the facts dispassionately, for I shall have done my duty to the utmost of my ability. . . .

I have always admired your amazing courage in the face of continual setbacks; in the way you have given me as good an education and background as anyone in the country; and always kept up appearances without ever losing faith in the future. My death would not mean that your struggle has been in vain. Far from it. It means that your sacrifice is as great as mine.

You must not grieve for me. . .I have no fear of death. . .The universe is so vast and so ageless that the life of one man can only be justified by the measure of his sacrifice. . .I am prepared to die with just one regret, and only one—that I could not devote myself to making your declining years more happy by being with you; but you will live in peace and freedom and I shall have directly contributed to that, so here again my life will not have been in vain.

Your loving son.

Shall I Compare Thee To a Summer's Day?

Shall I compare thee to a summer's day?
Thou art more lovely and more temperate:
Rough winds do shake the darling buds of May,
And summer's lease hath all too short a date:
Sometimes too hot the eye of heaven shines,
And often is his gold complexion dimm'd;
And every fair from fair sometimes declines,
By chance, or nature's changing course, untrimm'd;
But thy eternal summer shall not fade,
Nor lose possession of that fair thou owest;
Nor shall Death brag thou wander'st in his shade,
When in eternal lines to time thou growest;
So long as men can breathe, or eyes can see,
So long lives this, and this gives life to thee.

–William Shakespeare

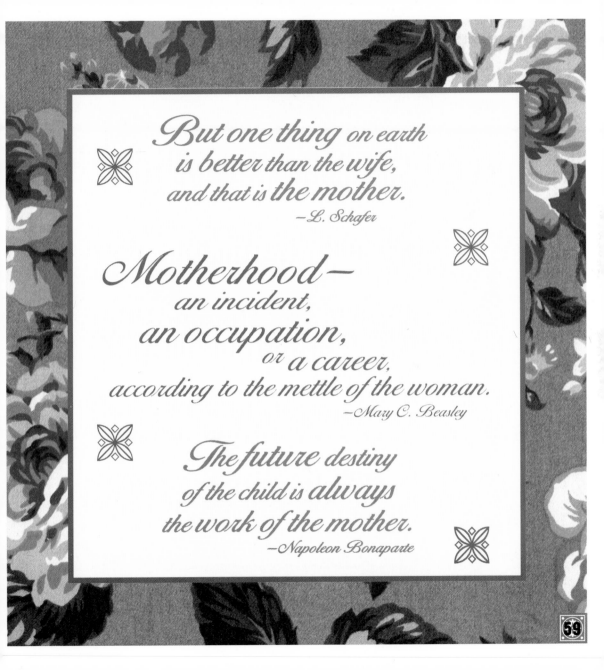

But one thing on earth
is better than the wife,
and that is **the mother.**
—*L. Schafer*

Motherhood —
an incident,
an occupation,
or a career,
according to the mettle of the woman.
—*Mary C. Beasley*

The future destiny
of the child is *always*
the work of the mother.
—*Napoleon Bonaparte*

MARCEL PROUST

Marcel Proust

Marcel Proust has been hailed as one of the most powerful and thought-provoking writers of his time. Born in 1871, his early life was sheltered by close ties with his mother. He was a spoiled and pampered child who had a hard time making friends. Bouts with asthma further contributed to his alienation and he retreated into a private world of thoughts. His greatest work, *Remembrances of Things Past*, searches the boundaries of memory through recreations of experience, and it was his sensitive analysis of human emotions which gained him high praise from France's leading thinkers near the end of his life.

To feel, to love, to suffer, and to devote herself
will always be the text of a woman's life.
– Honore de Balzac

December 1903

My dear little Mama,

I can't sleep, so I'm writing this note to tell you that I'm thinking of you. I would so much like, I so much want, to be able soon to get up at the same time as you do and drink my breakfast coffee with you. To feel our sleep and our waking distributed over the same hours would be, will be, such a delight to me. . . .Forgive me for leaving the smoking room in disorder.

I was working hard up to the last moment. And as for this beautiful envelope, it's the only one I had. Make Marie and Antoine keep quiet and keep the kitchen door closed, so their voices don't come through.

A thousand loving kisses,

Marcel

I feel that I will sleep very well now.

Nature

As a fond mother, when the day is o'er,
Leads by the hand her little child to bed,
Half willing, half reluctant to be led,
And leave his broken playthings on the floor,
Still gazing at them through the open door
Not wholly reassured and comforted
By promises of others in their stead,
Which, though more splendid, may not please him more;
So Nature deals with us, and takes away
Our playthings one by one, and by the hand
Leads us to rest so gently, that we go
Scarce knowing if we wish to go or stay,
Being too full of sleep to understand
How far the unknown transcends the what we know.

–Henry Wadsworth Longfellow

God could not be everywhere,
therefore he made mothers.
— *Jewish Proverb*

The greatest love is a mother's.
— *Polish Proverb*

Mother — that was the bank
where we deposited
all our hurts and worries.
— *Anonymous*

Robert Schumann

Robert Schumann

Robert Schumann (1810-1856) was an important German composer and pianist who had a legendary romantic style and a passionate love of literature. His talent for combining the beauty of music with the written word was sensitive and as a result, his symphonies endure in popularity and his piano pieces continue to be rigorously studied. The following letter to his mother is one of several kind notes the mother and son exchanged throughout the course of their lives.

The successful mother sets her children free and becomes more free herself in the process.
—Robert J. Havighurst

Heidelberg
July 30, 1830 5am

Good morning Mamma!

How shall I describe my bliss at this moment: the spirit-lamp is hissing under the coffee-pot, the sky is indescribably clear and rosy, and the keen spirit of the morning fills me with its presence. Besides, your letter lies before me and reveals a perfect treasury of good feeling, common sense, and virtue. My cigar tastes uncommonly good; in short, the world is very lovely at times, if one only could always get up early. . . .

Good-bye, dear Mother, and do not fret. In this case Heaven will only help us if we help ourselves.

Ever your most loving son,

Robert Schumann

The First Time

I wish I could remember the first day,
First hour, first moment of your meeting me;
If bright or dim the season, it might be
Summer or winter for aught I can say.
So unrecorded did it slip away,
So blind was I to see and to foresee,
So dull to mark the budding of my tree
That would not blossom yet for many a May.
If only I could recollect it! Such
A day of days! I let it come and go
As traceless as a thaw of bygone snow.
It seemed to mean so little, meant so much!
If only now I could recall that touch,
First hand of hand in hand! — Did one but know!

—Christina Rossetti

*Every mother of more than one child
has a secret favorite,
so secret that she might go through her
whole life and never admit to herself
which one it was.*

— Gail Godwin

*You don't choose your family,
They are God's gift to you,
as you are to them.*

— Desmond Tutu

*The finest inheritance you
can give to a child is to allow
it to make its own way,
completely on its own feet.*

— Isadora Duncan

GUSTAVE FLAUBERT

Gustave Flaubert

Gustave Flaubert (1821-1880) was an influential nineteenth century author, whose most famous work of prose was The Temptation of St. Anthony. This work, one of only five major writings during his

lifetime, brought him long-awaited recognition from his family and the French aristocracy and earned him a prominent position in European literary history. Throughout his life, Flaubert maintained a deeply personal relationship with his mother. The following letter was written in response to her questioning when he would marry.

My mother was the most beautiful woman I ever saw.
– George Washington

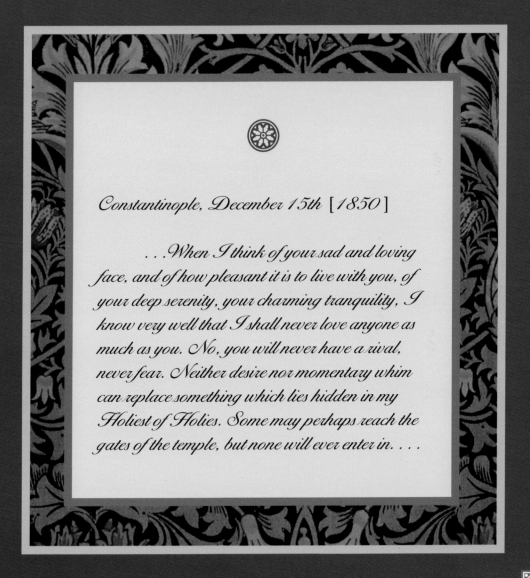

Constantinople, December 15th [1850]

. . .When I think of your sad and loving face, and of how pleasant it is to live with you, of your deep serenity, your charming tranquility, I know very well that I shall never love anyone as much as you. No, you will never have a rival, never fear. Neither desire nor momentary whim can replace something which lies hidden in my Holiest of Holies. Some may perhaps reach the gates of the temple, but none will ever enter in. . . .

How Do I Love Thee?

How do I love thee? Let me count the ways.
I love thee to the depth and breadth and height
My soul can reach, when feeling out of sight
For the ends of Being and ideal Grace.
I love thee to the level of everyday's
Most quiet need, by sun and candle-light.
I love thee freely, as men strive for Right;
I love thee purely, as they turn from Praise.
I love thee with the passion put to use
In my old griefs, and with my childhood's faith.
I love thee with a love I seemed to lose
With my lost saints, — I love thee with the breath,
Smiles, tears, of all my life! — and, if God choose,
I shall but love thee better after death.

—Elizabeth Barrett Browning

A child without
a mother is like
a door without a knob.
— Jewish Proverb

Life is the first gift,
love is the second,
& *understanding* the third.
— Marge Piercy

The toughest part of **motherhood**
is the **inner worrying**
and **not showing it.**
— Audrey Hepburn

Any mother could
perform the jobs of several
air traffic controllers with ease.
— Lisa Alther

SYLVIA PLATH

Sylvia Plath

Sylvia Plath, renowned author, gained enormous appreciation very early in her literary career. Born in Boston in 1932, she received high praise for technical merit in her first volume of prose, Colossus. Plath's writings deal with the contrasts between extreme states of mind. To a large extent, these writings were autobiographical. In real life, Plath dealt daily with the effects of her own mental instability. Throughout years of mental problems, her mother was a source of continual support and, encouragement. A large body of correspondence such as the following note, existed between the two women.

> Who ran to help me when I fell,
> And would some pretty story tell,
> Or kiss the place to make it well?
> My mother.
> —Ann Taylor

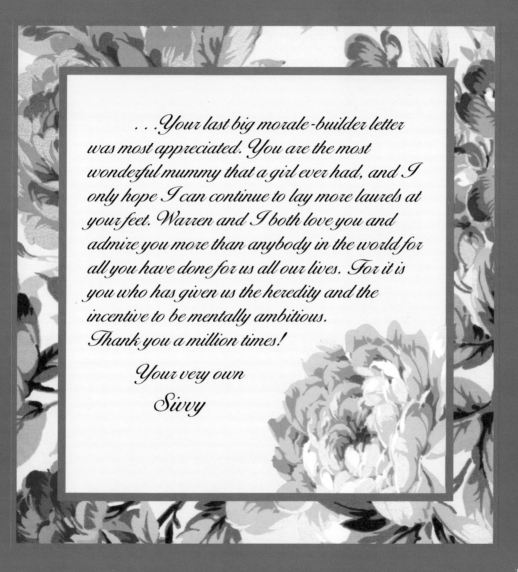

. . . Your last big morale-builder letter was most appreciated. You are the most wonderful mummy that a girl ever had, and I only hope I can continue to lay more laurels at your feet. Warren and I both love you and admire you more than anybody in the world for all you have done for us all our lives. For it is you who has given us the heredity and the incentive to be mentally ambitious. Thank you a million times!

Your very own

Sivvy

There Is Always a Place For You

There is always a place for you at my table,
You never need to be invited.
I'll share every crust as long as I'm able,
And know you will be delighted.
There is always a place for you by my fire,
And though it may burn to embers,
If warmth and good cheer are your desire
The friend of your heart remembers!
There is always a place for you by my side,
And should the years tear us apart,
I will face lonely moments more satisfied
With a place for you in my heart!

—Anne Campbell

I think my life began with waking up & loving my mother's face.

—George Eliot

*Love them,
feed them,
discipline them
and let them go free.
You may have a life-long
good relationship.*

—Mary G. L. Davis

To forget one's ancestors is to be a brook without a source, a tree without a root.

—Chinese Proverb

LOUIS BRANDEIS

Louis Brandeis

Louis Brandeis (1856-1941) was a staunch Supreme Court Justice whose social and economic theories have had a lasting impact on American legal history. Brandeis was a true humanitarian, often volunteering legal services at no charge to worthy causes. Throughout his life, Brandeis often attributed his success to his mother. The following letter is an affectionate example of their relationship.

If in life you may have friends fond, dear friends, but never will you have again the inexpressible love and gentleness lavished upon you which none but a Mother bestows.
—Macaulay

November 12, 1888

    I must send you another birthday greeting and tell you how much I love you; that with each day I learn to extol your love and your worth more—and that when I look back over my life, I can find nothing in your treatment of me that I would alter. You often said, dearest mother, that I find fault—but I always told you candidly that I felt and sought to change only that little which appeared to me to be possible of improvement. I believe, most beloved mother, that the improvement of the world, reform, can only arise when mothers like you are increased thousands of times and have more children.

✿   ✿   ✿

An Hour With Thee!

An hour with thee! When earliest day
Dapples with gold the eastern grey,
Oh, what can frame my mind to bear
The toil and turmoil, cark and care,
New griefs, which coming hours unfold,
And sad remembrance of the old?
One hour with thee.

One hour with thee! When burning June
Waves his red flag at pitch of noon;
What shall repay the faithful swain,
His labour on the sultry plain;
And, more than cave or sheltering bough,
Cool feverish blood and throbbing brow?
One hour with thee.

One hour with thee! When sun is set,
Oh, what can teach me to forget
The thankless labours of the day;
The hopes, the wishes, flung away;
The increasing wants, and lessening gains,
The master's pride, who scorns my pains?
One hour with thee.

—Sir Walter Scott

Mother is the name for God
in the lips and hearts of children.
—William Makepeace Thackeray

If you want your children to turn out well,
spend twice as much time with them,
and **half as much money**.
—Abigail Van Buren

There are only two **things** a child
will share willingly —
communicable diseases and his *mother's* age.
—Benjamin Spock

KATHERINE MANSFIELD

Katherine Mansfield

Katherine Mansfield is best known as a master storyteller, famous for her short stories which wove delicate patterns around complex characters. Katherine lived in London, where she often contributed to a variety of periodicals and journals. In 1918 she married critic John Middleton Murry and became a part of the literary circle which included luminaries such as D. H. Lawrence and Virginia Woolf. Her relationship with her mother, who was often ill, was a caring and compassionate one. The two women often corresponded through their long letters. The following letter is one of many exchanged between Katherine and her mother.

. . .there is nothing so strong as the force of love; there is no love so forcible as the love of an affectionate mother to her natural child.
—Elizabeth Grymeston

Rose Tree Cottage / The Lee / Great Missenden / Buckinghamshire
December 15, 1914

My darling little Mother,

How terrible that you should have been ill again, and so severely ill. Do you know I have had an extraordinary presentiment that something was happening to you? Every evening when my work was done and I sat down by the fire I felt your nearness and your dearness to me and such love for you in my heart and such a longing to hold you in my arms that I could have cried like a baby. The only way to cure my sadness was to talk about you to Jack and make him see you, too. I really believe (with all the going into the silence nonsense aside) that you and I are curiously near to each other. I feel through you so much and I dream of you so vividly. Oh, my little precious brave Mother, if my love can help you to get strong you are better now. My heart yearns over you. I see you in bed with your pretty hands crossed and your springy hair on the pillow and I cannot come in and ask if you feel inclined for a little powwow. I am quite well and strong again, but I pray that you are better and that you are going to have a happy Xmas and a New Year full of the blessings that you deserve. . . .

My dear darling. Here is a little handkerchief which looks like you, to me. Bless you always. I simply devoured your letters. I am always your own devoted child.

Mother

You painted no Madonnas
On chapel walls in Rome;
But, with a touch diviner,
Upon the walls of home.

You wrote no lofty poems
With rare poetic art;
But with a finer vision,
You put poems in my heart.

You carved no shapeless marble
To symmetry divine;
But, with a nobler genius,
You shaped this soul of mine.

You built no great cathedrals,
The centuries applaud;
But, with a grace exquisite,
Your heart was house of God.

Had I the gift of Raphael,
Or Michael Angelo,
Oh, what a rare Madonna
My mother's life would show.

—Thomas W. Fessenden

*My mother loved children —
she would have given anything
if I had been one.*
— Groucho Marx

*All the earth, though it were
full of kind hearts,
is but a desolation and a
desert place to mother
when her only child is absent.*
— Elizabeth Gaskell

*Of all the rights of women,
the greatest is to be a mother.*
— Lin Yutang

To order additional copies of this book, write:

PENBROOKE PUBLISHING
P.O. Box 700566
Tulsa, OK 74170